Swear Word Coloring Book

SwearWord Adult Coloring Book

Deep In The Sweary Ocean
(Rude Sea Creatures)

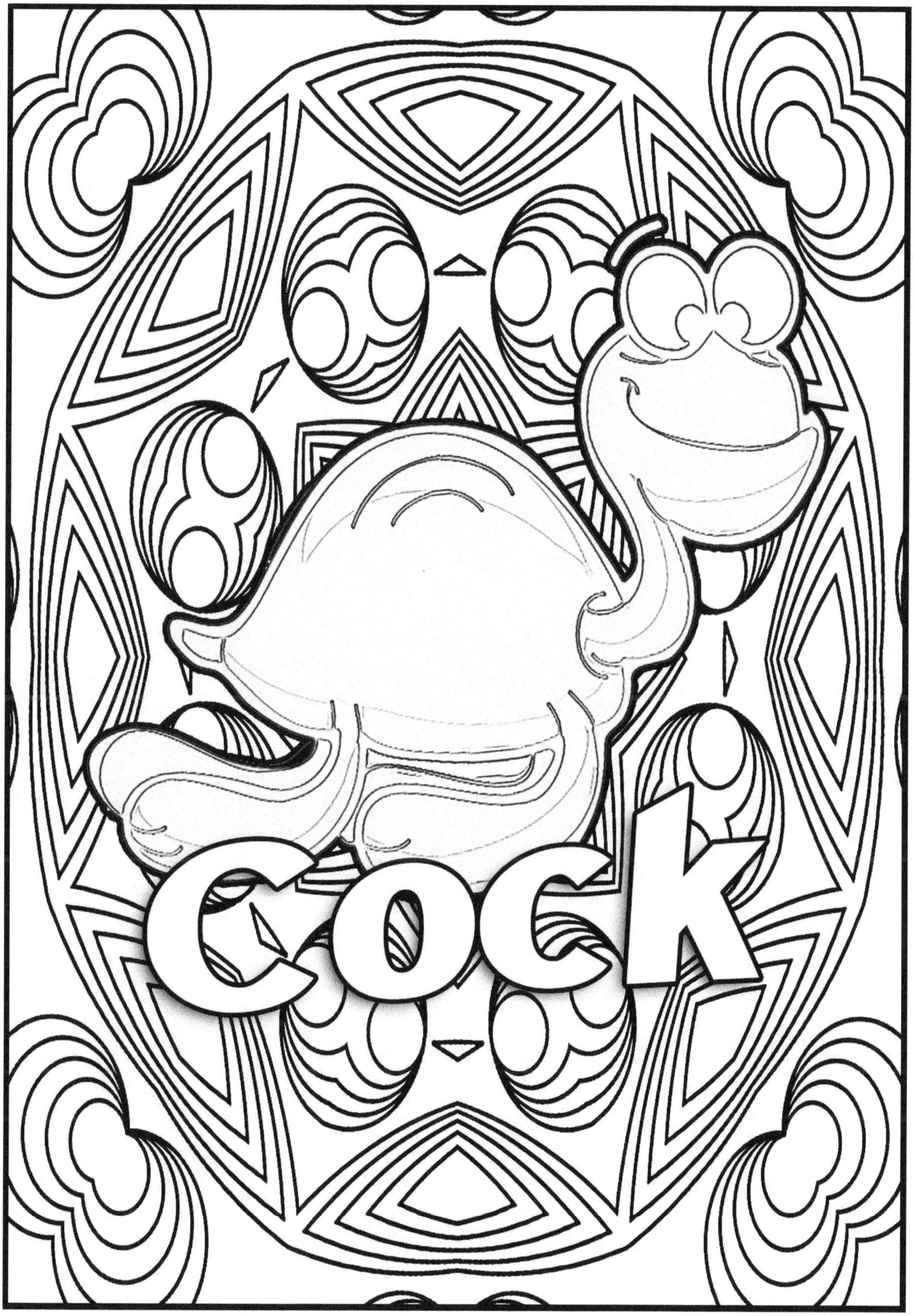
Cock

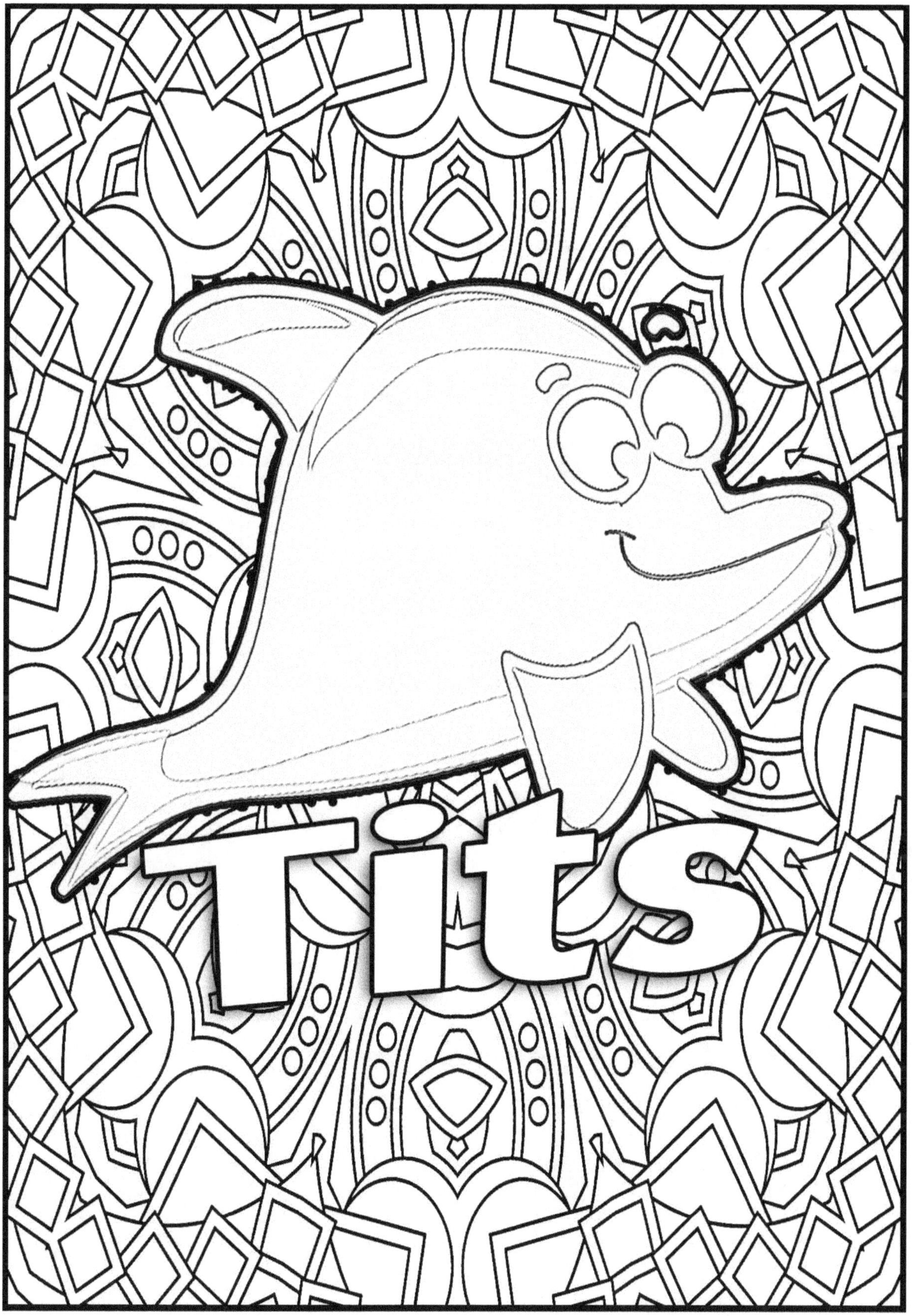
Tits

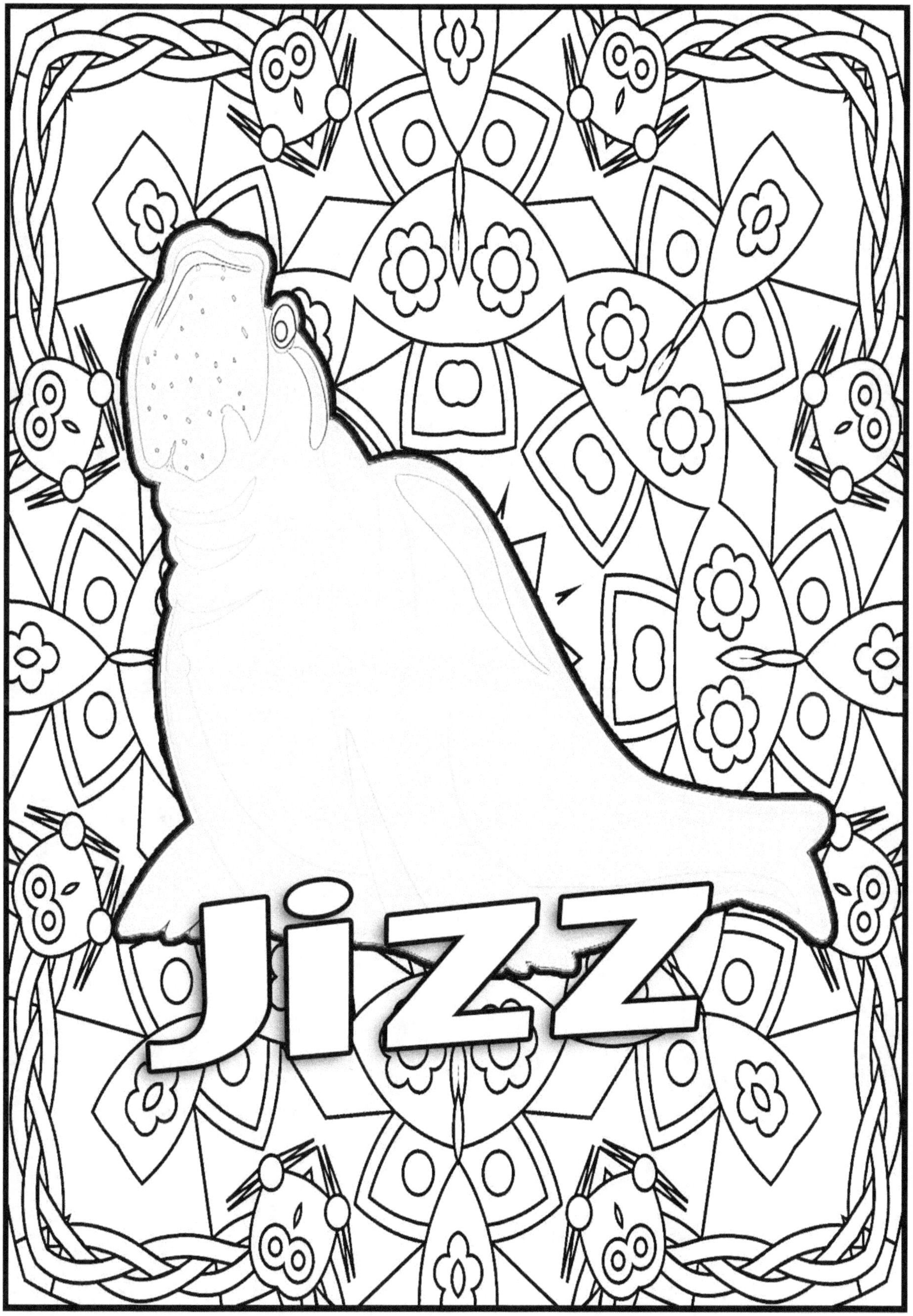
JIZZ

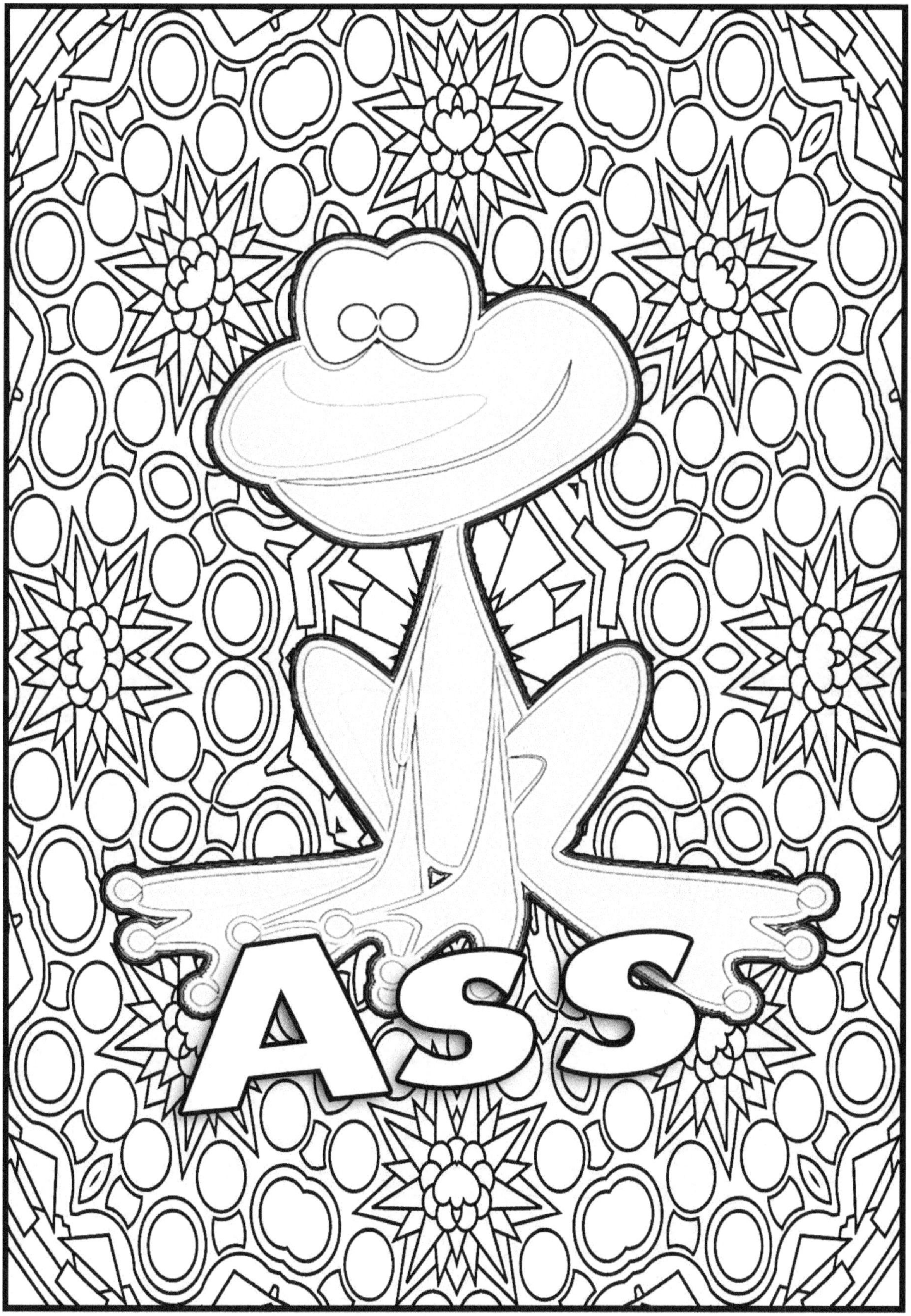
ASS

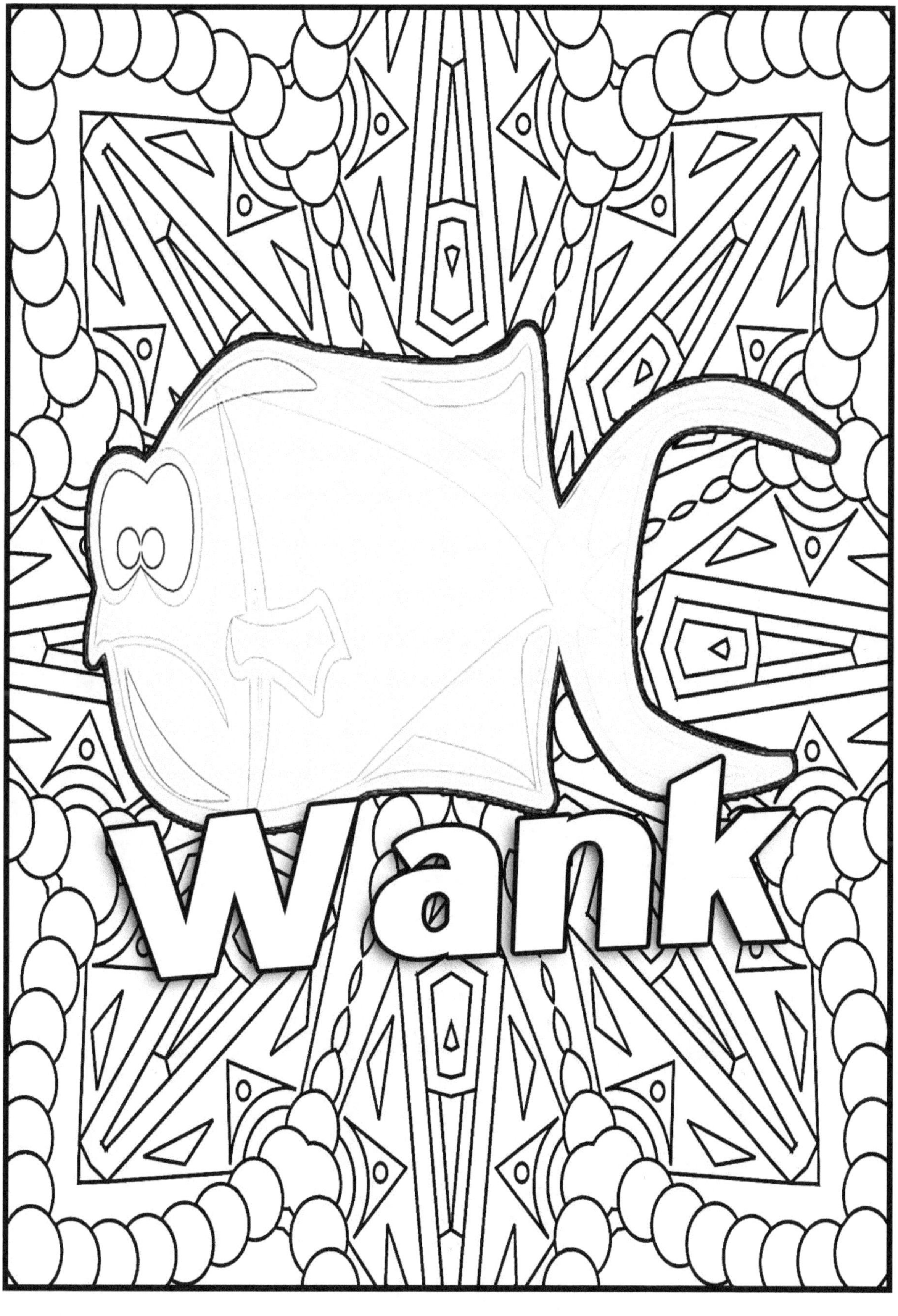
Wank

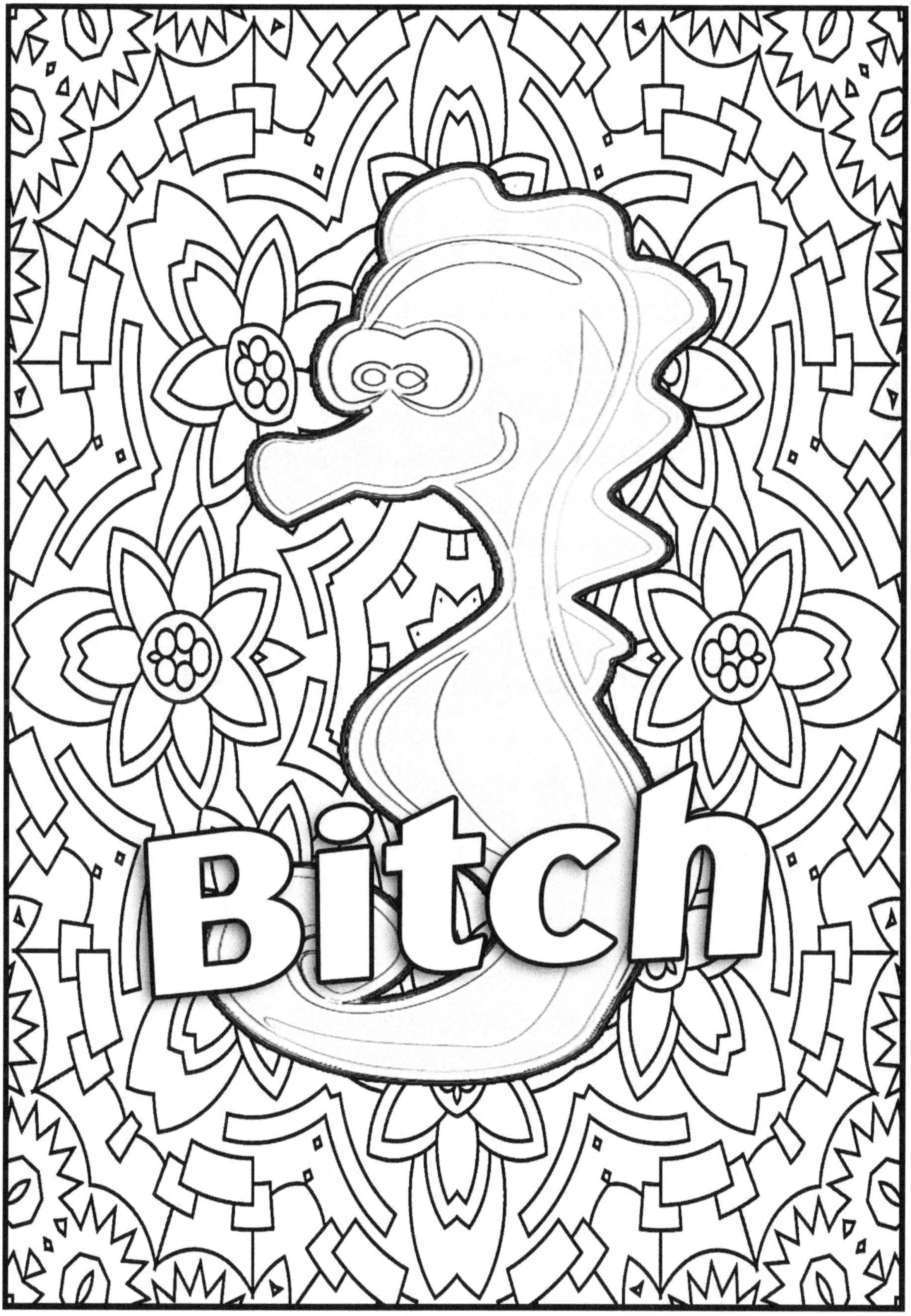
Bitch

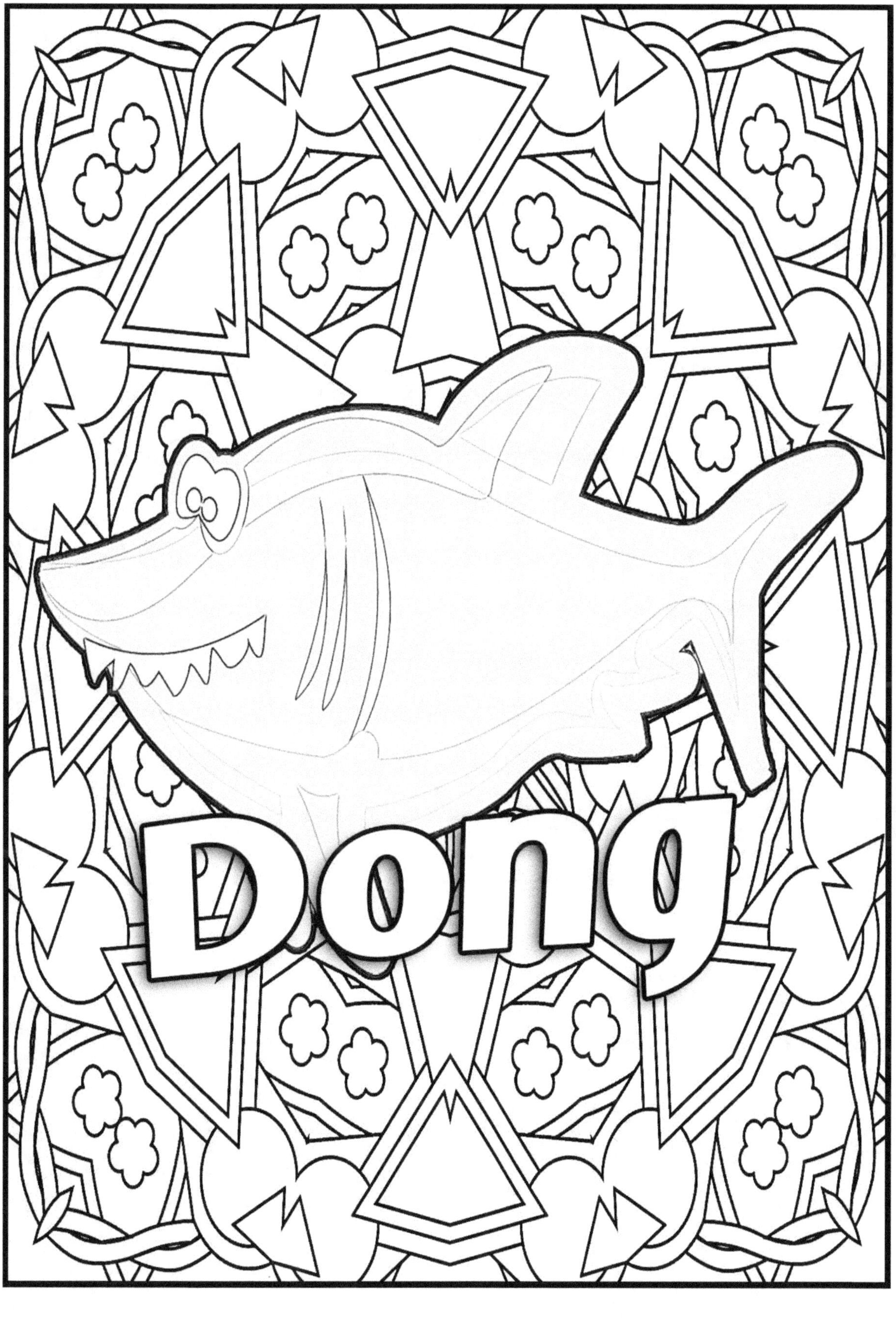
Dong

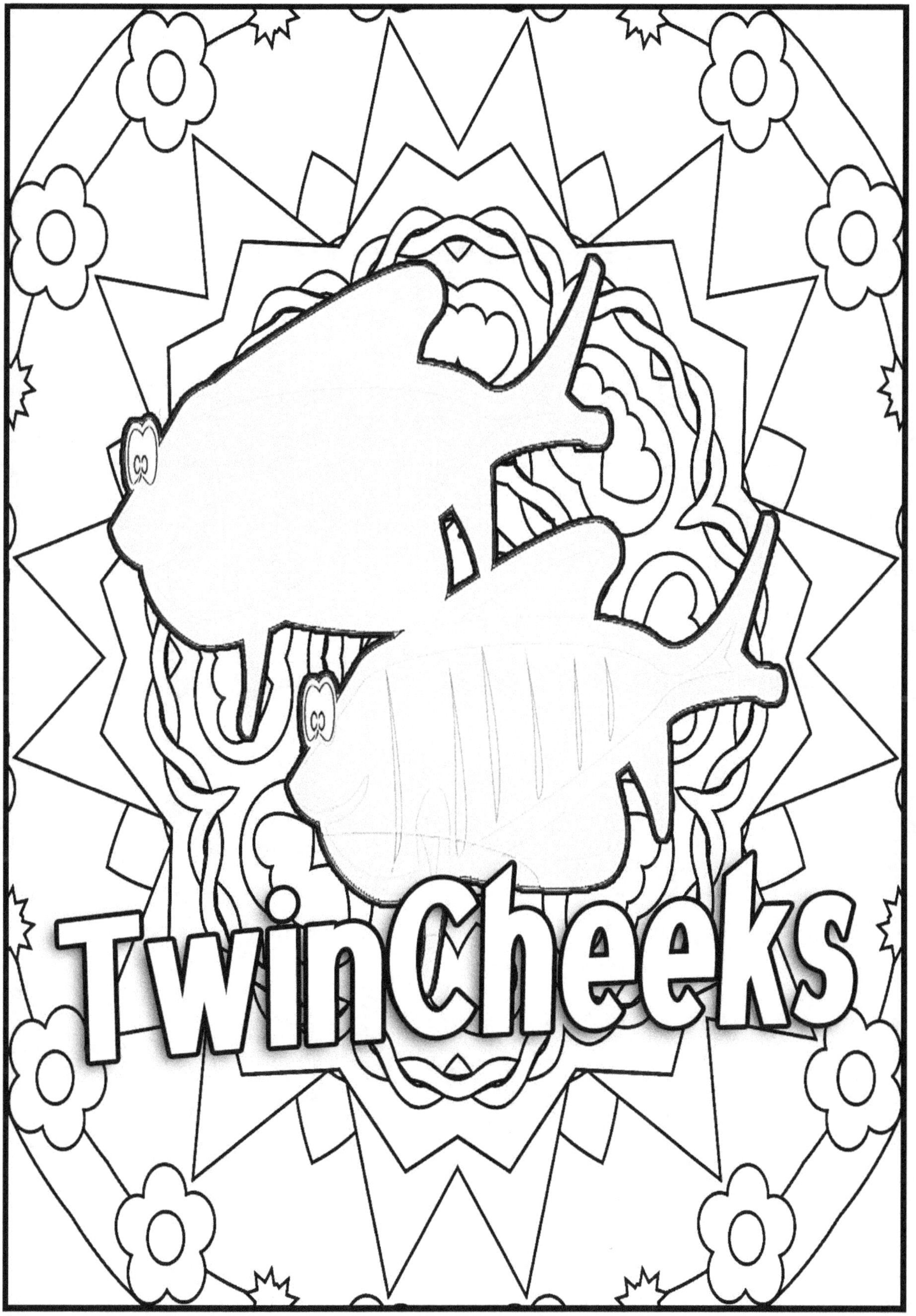
TwinCheeks

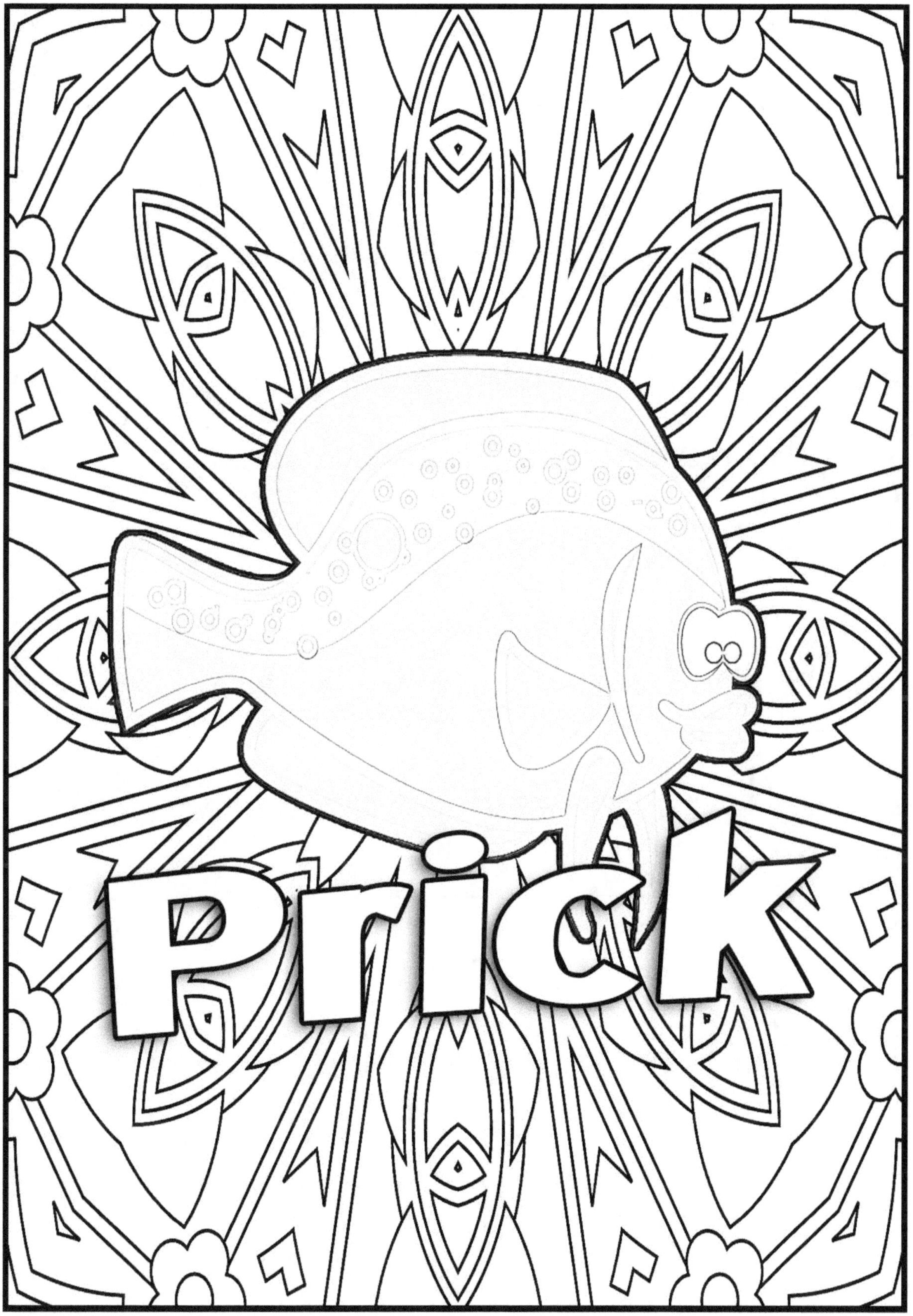
Prick

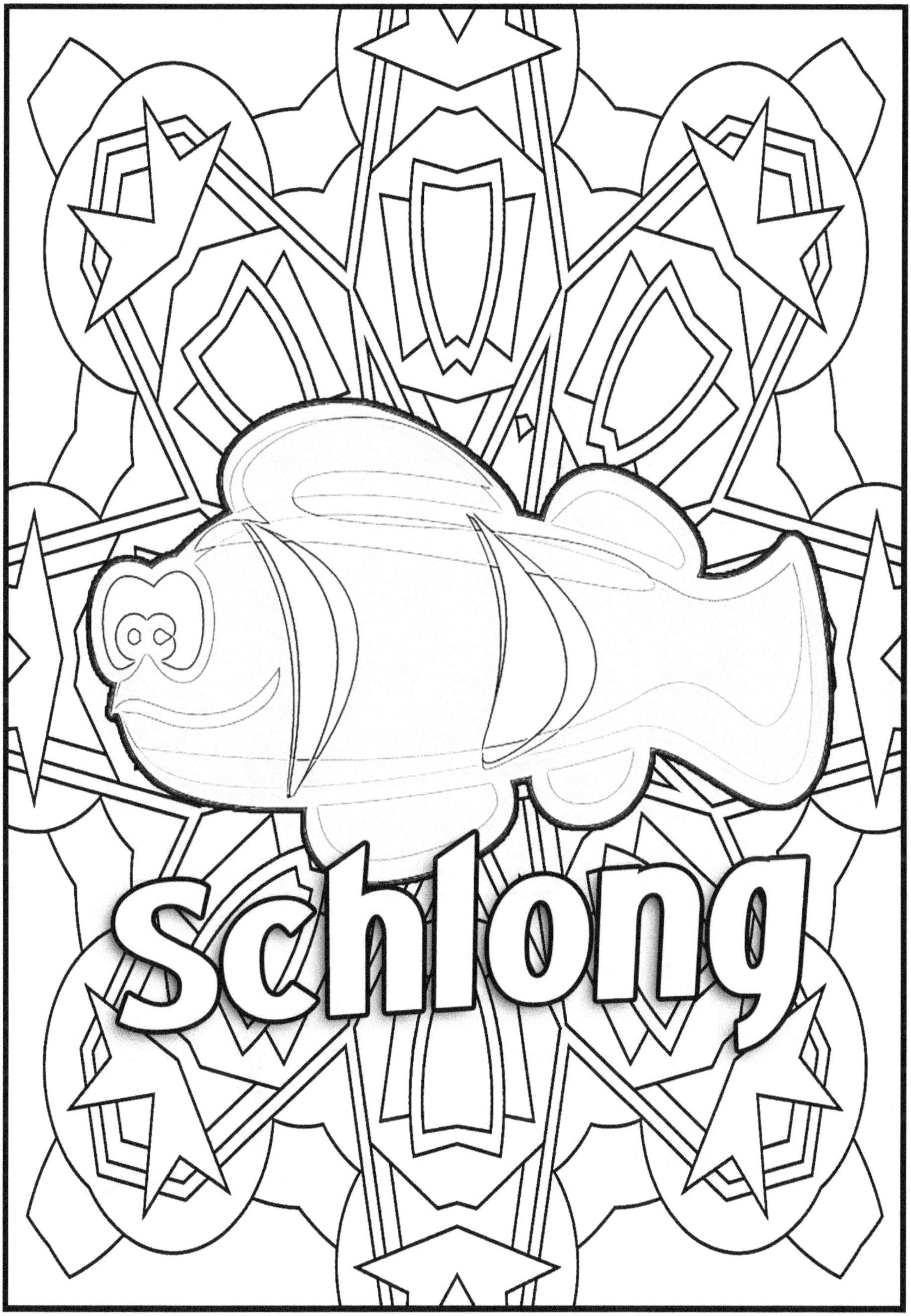
Schlong

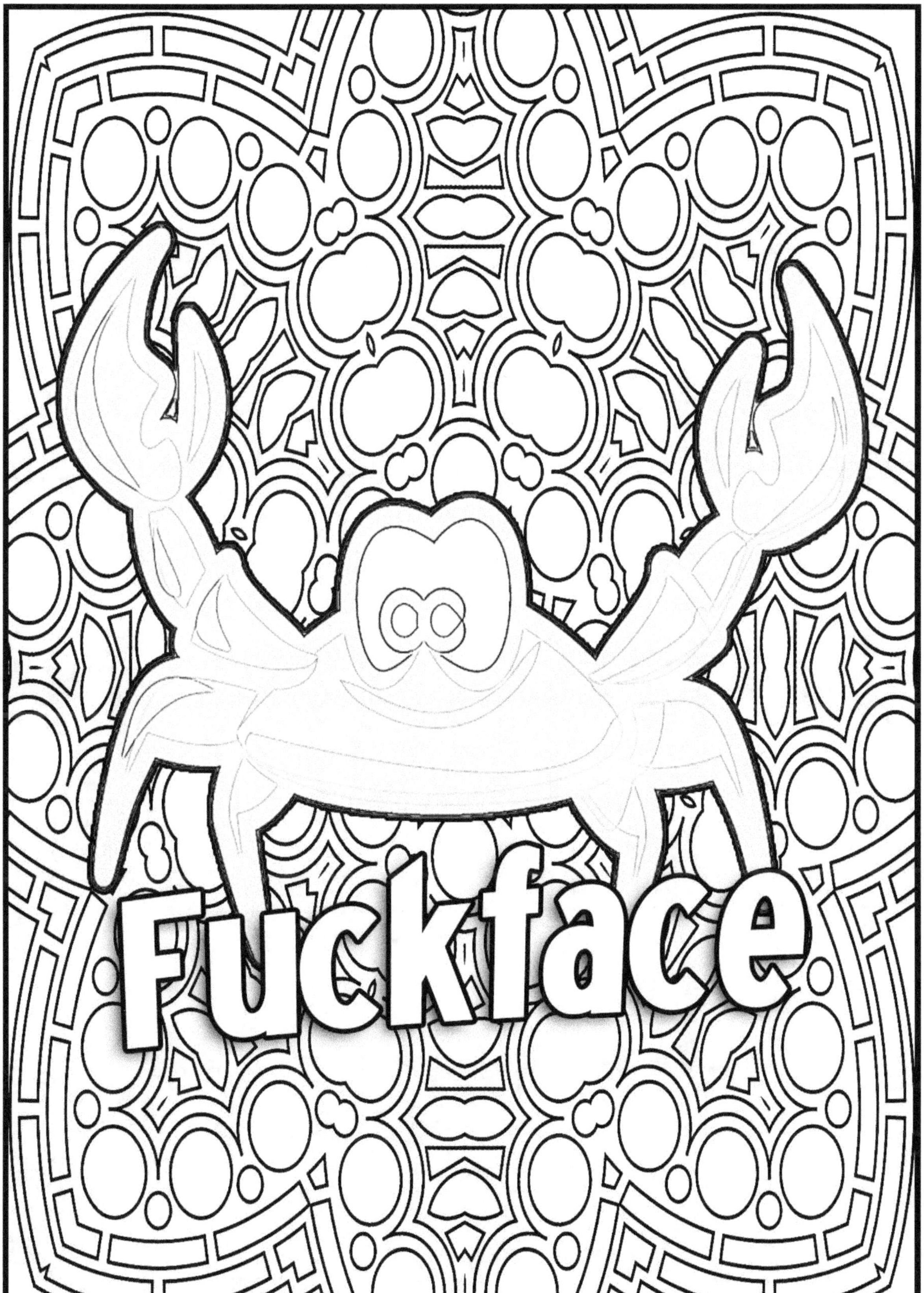
Fuckface

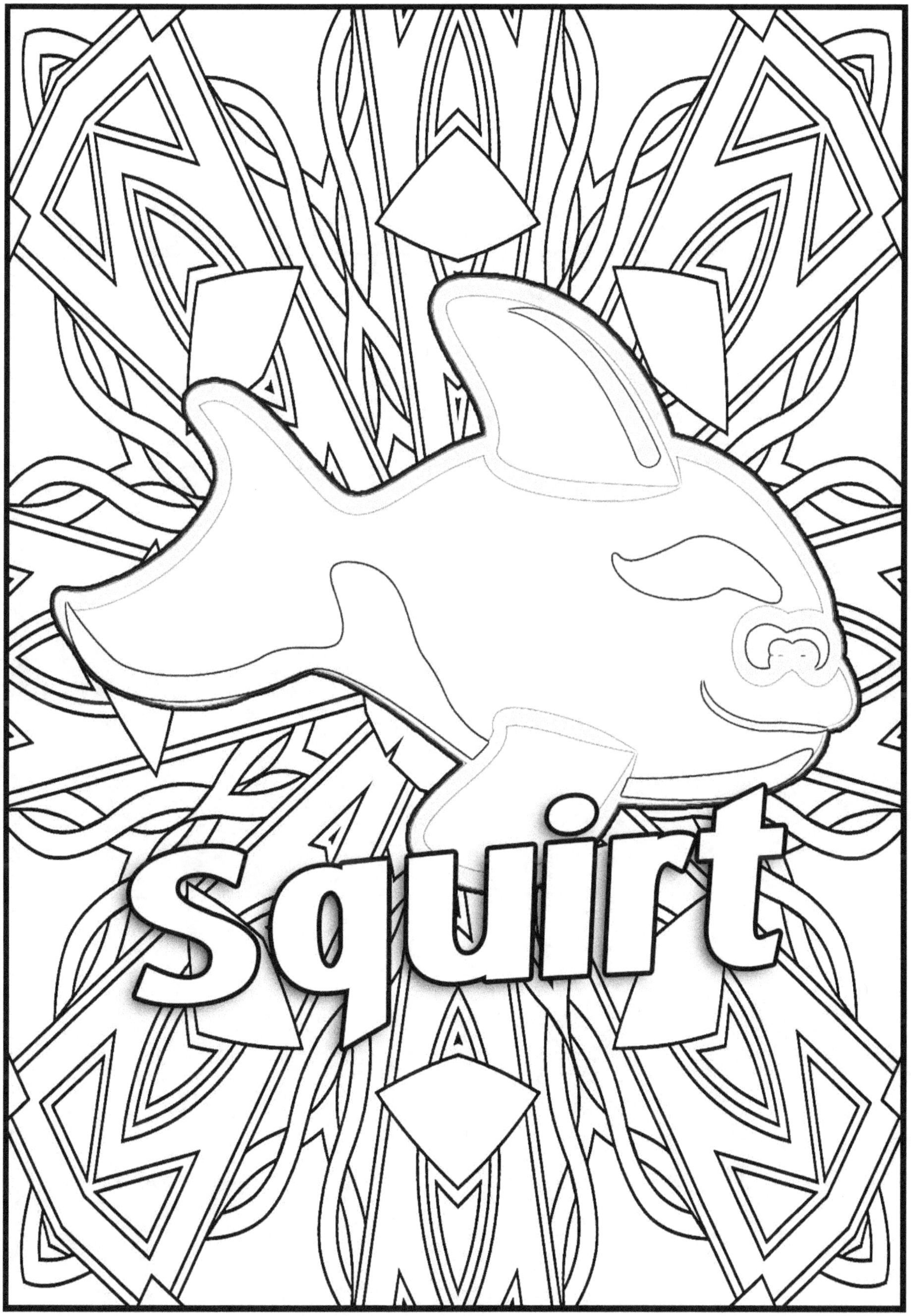
Squirt

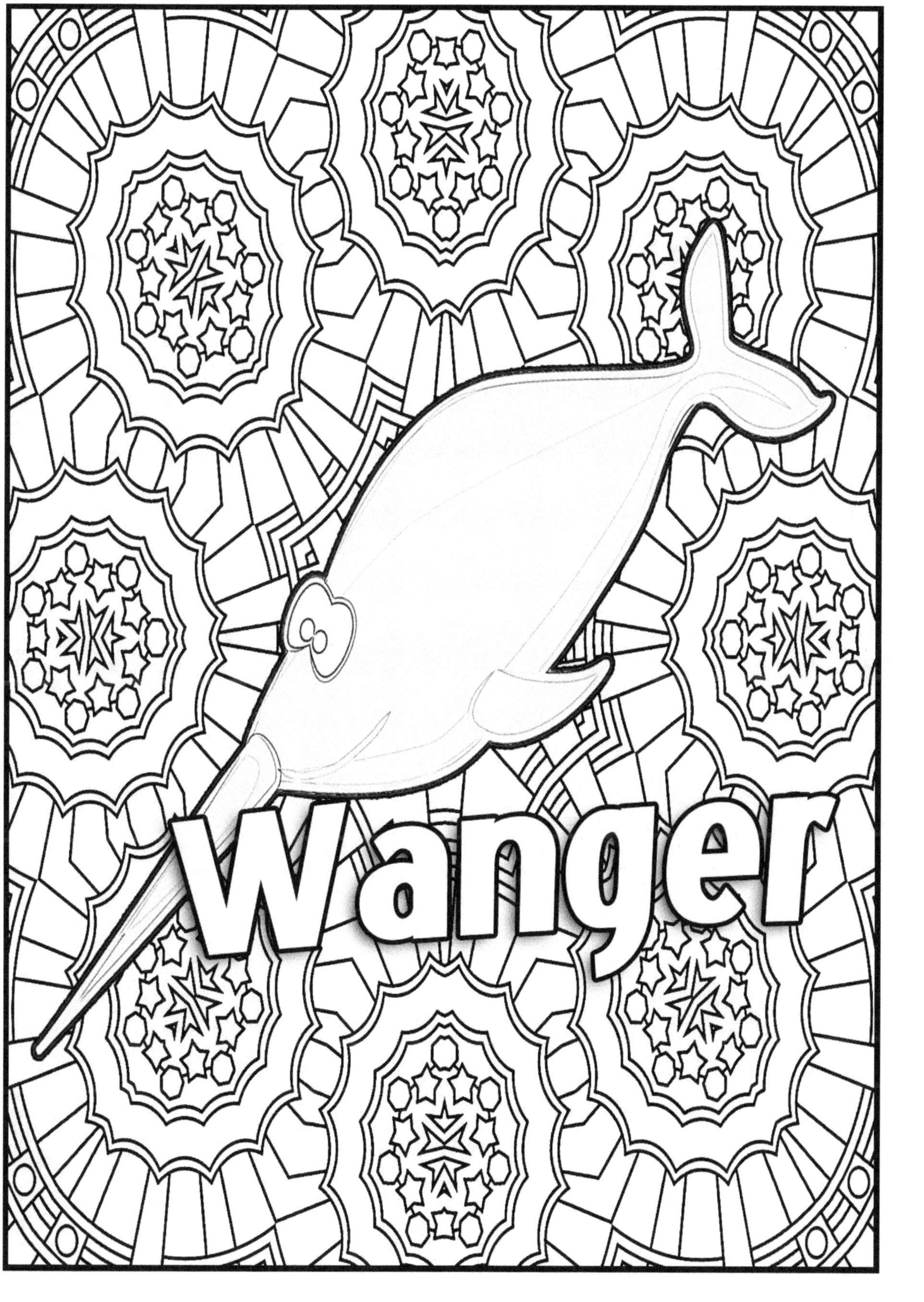
Wanger

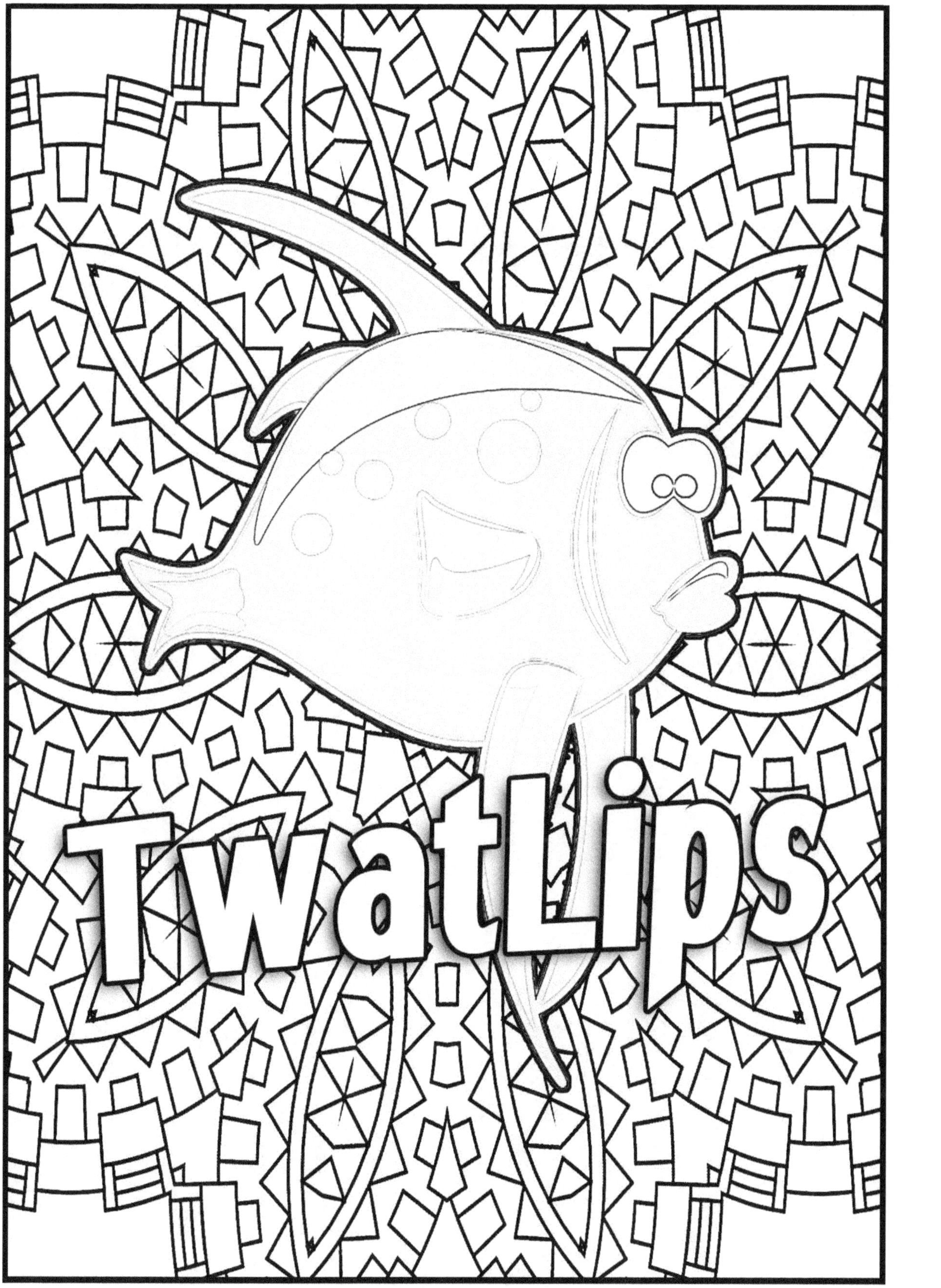
TwatLips

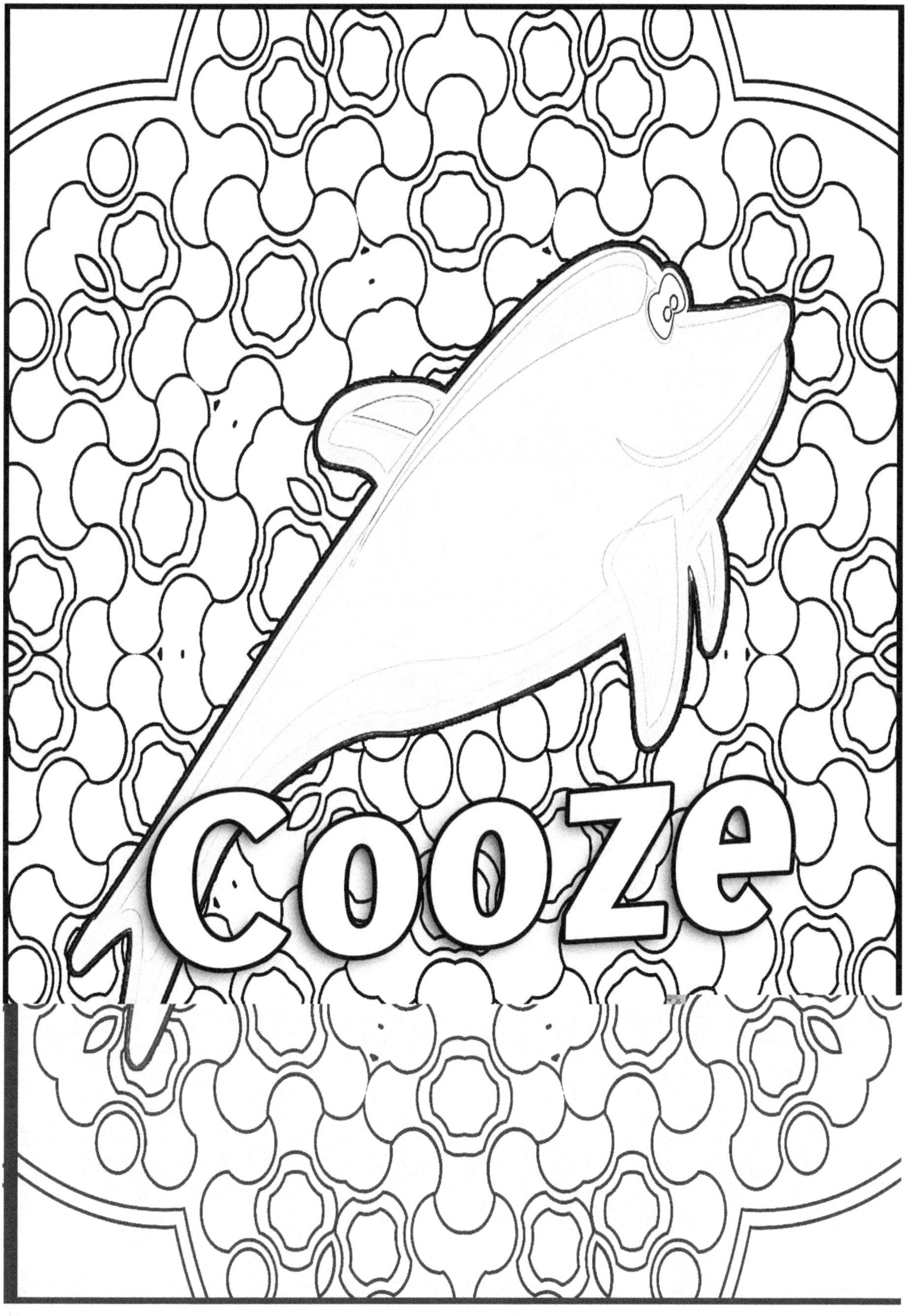
Cooze

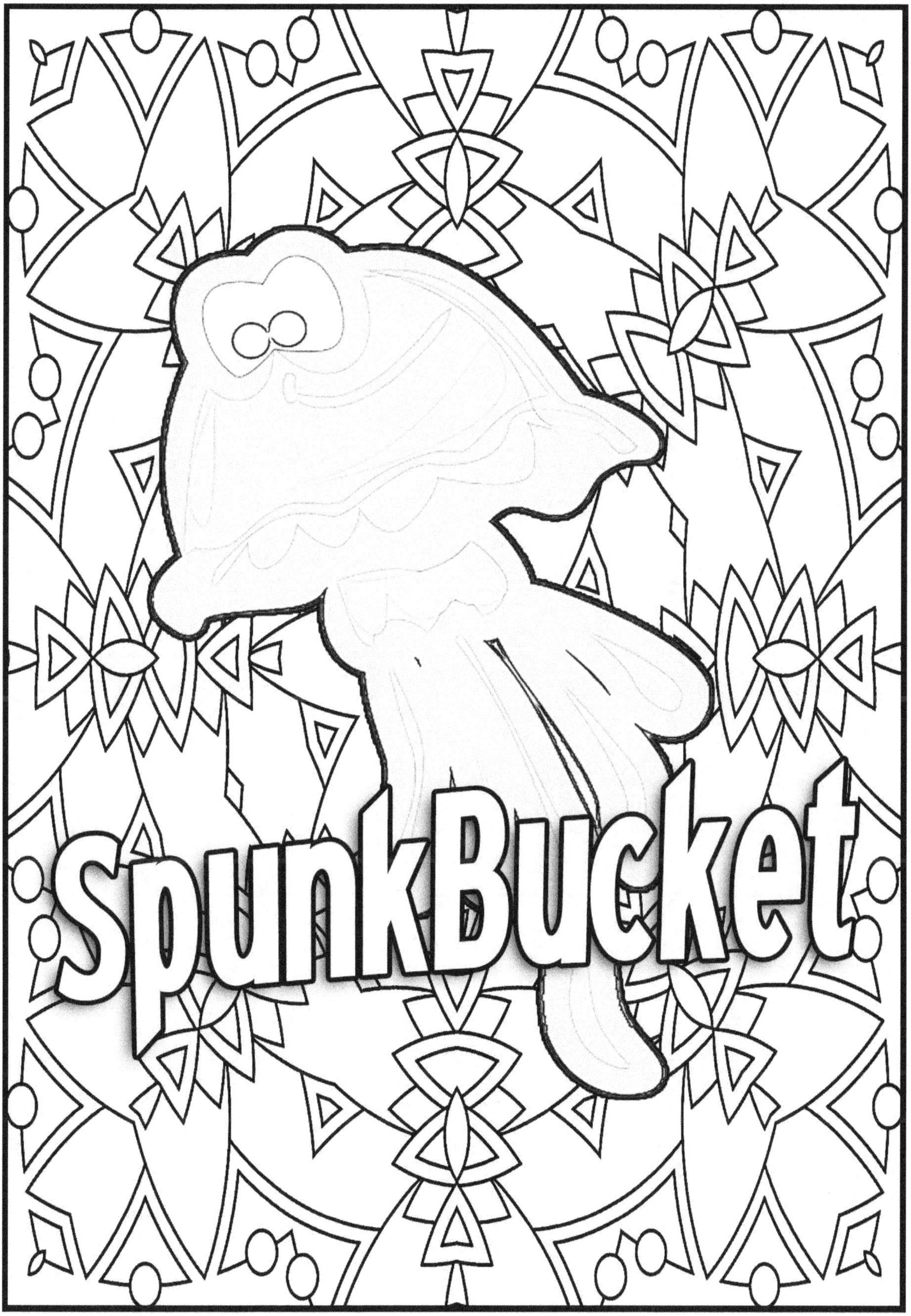
SpunkBucket

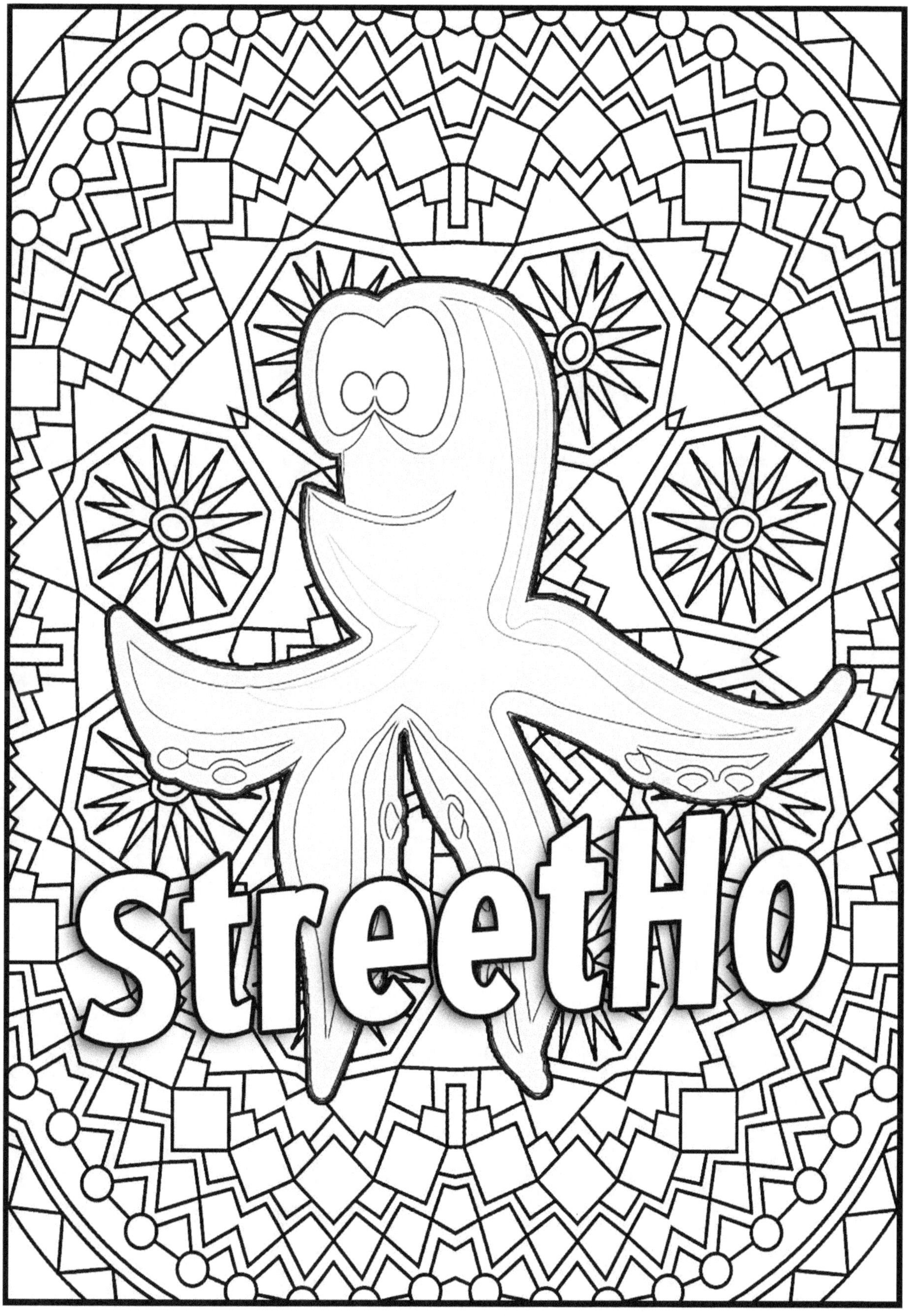
StreetHO

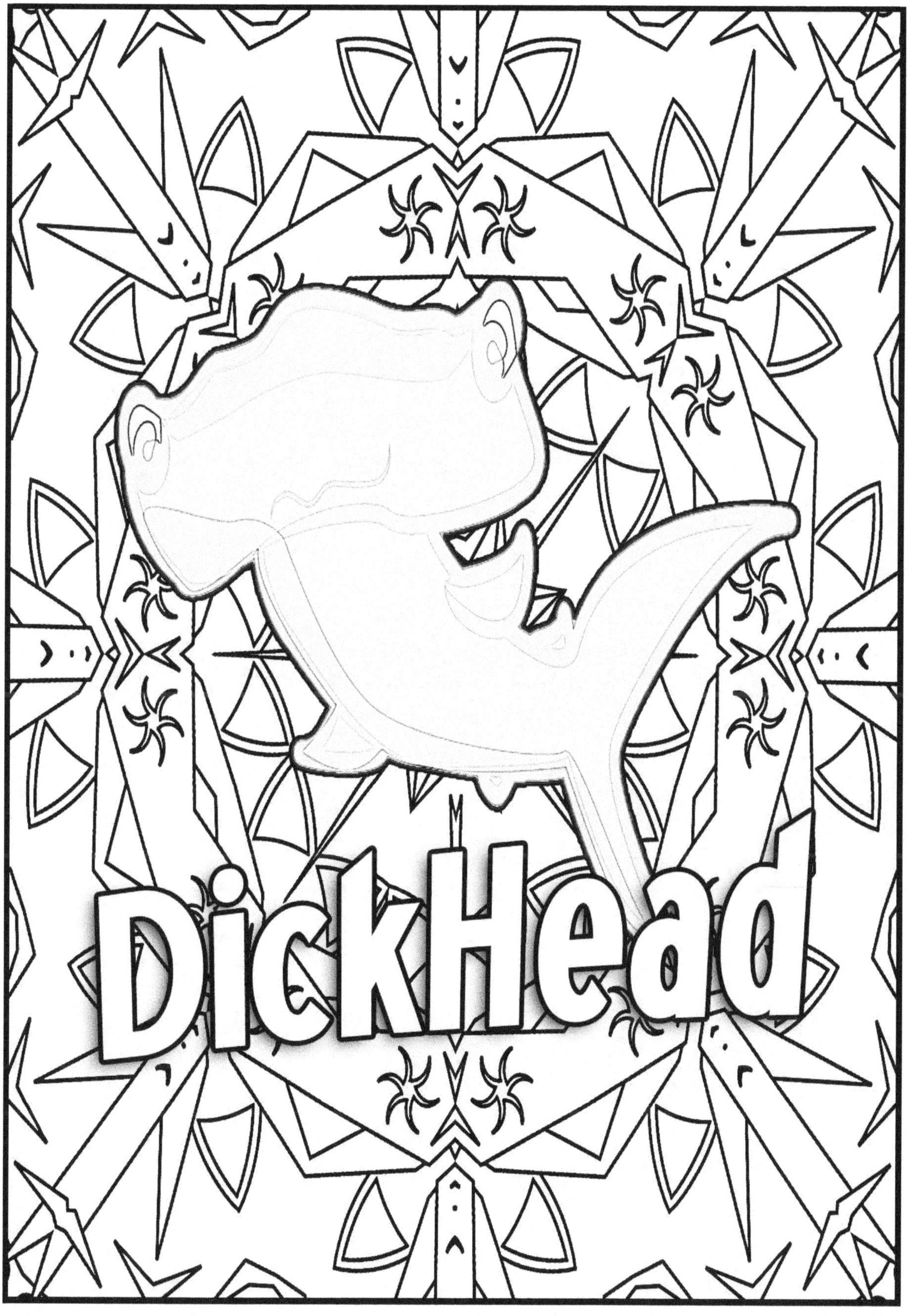
DickHead

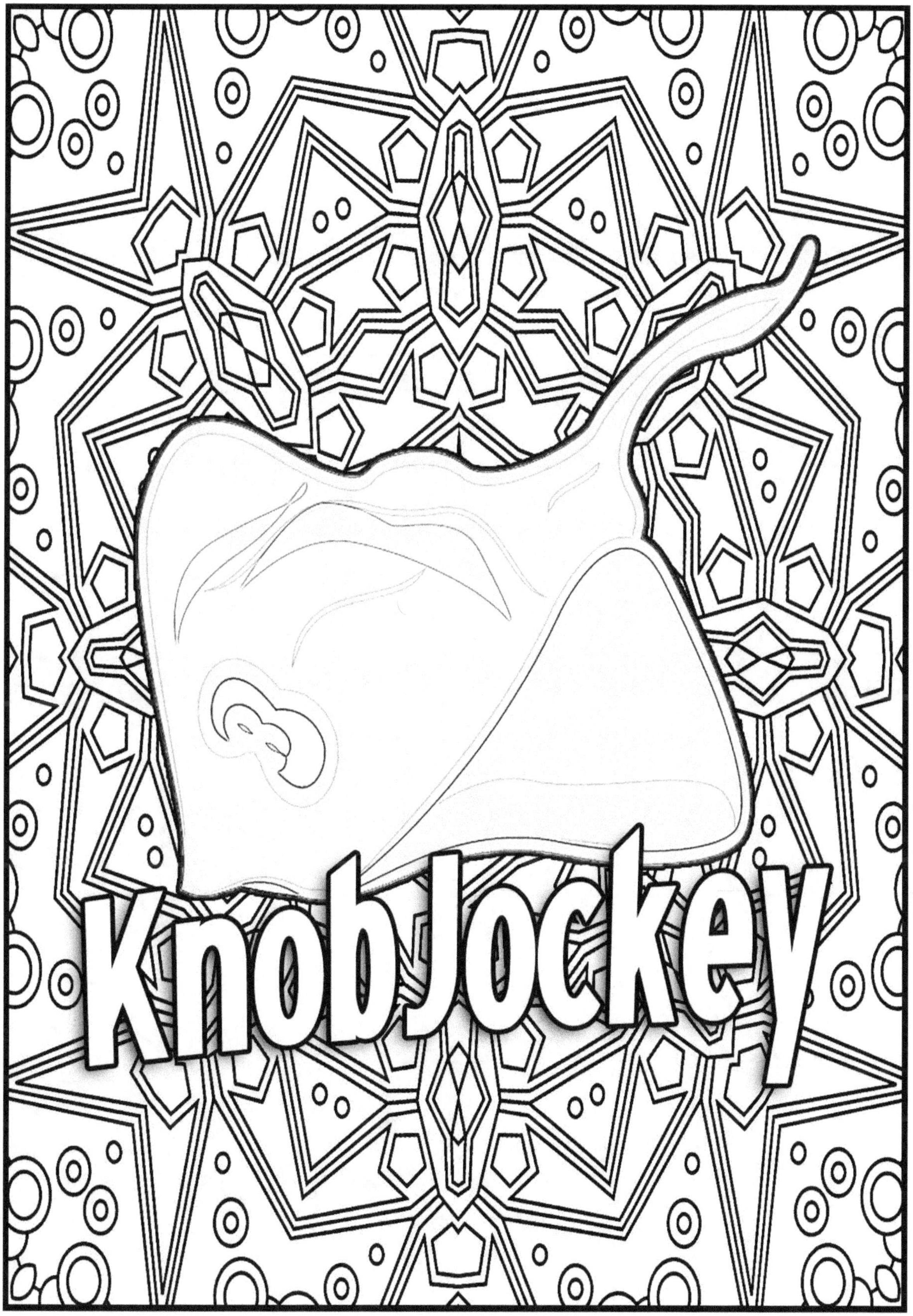
Knob Jockey

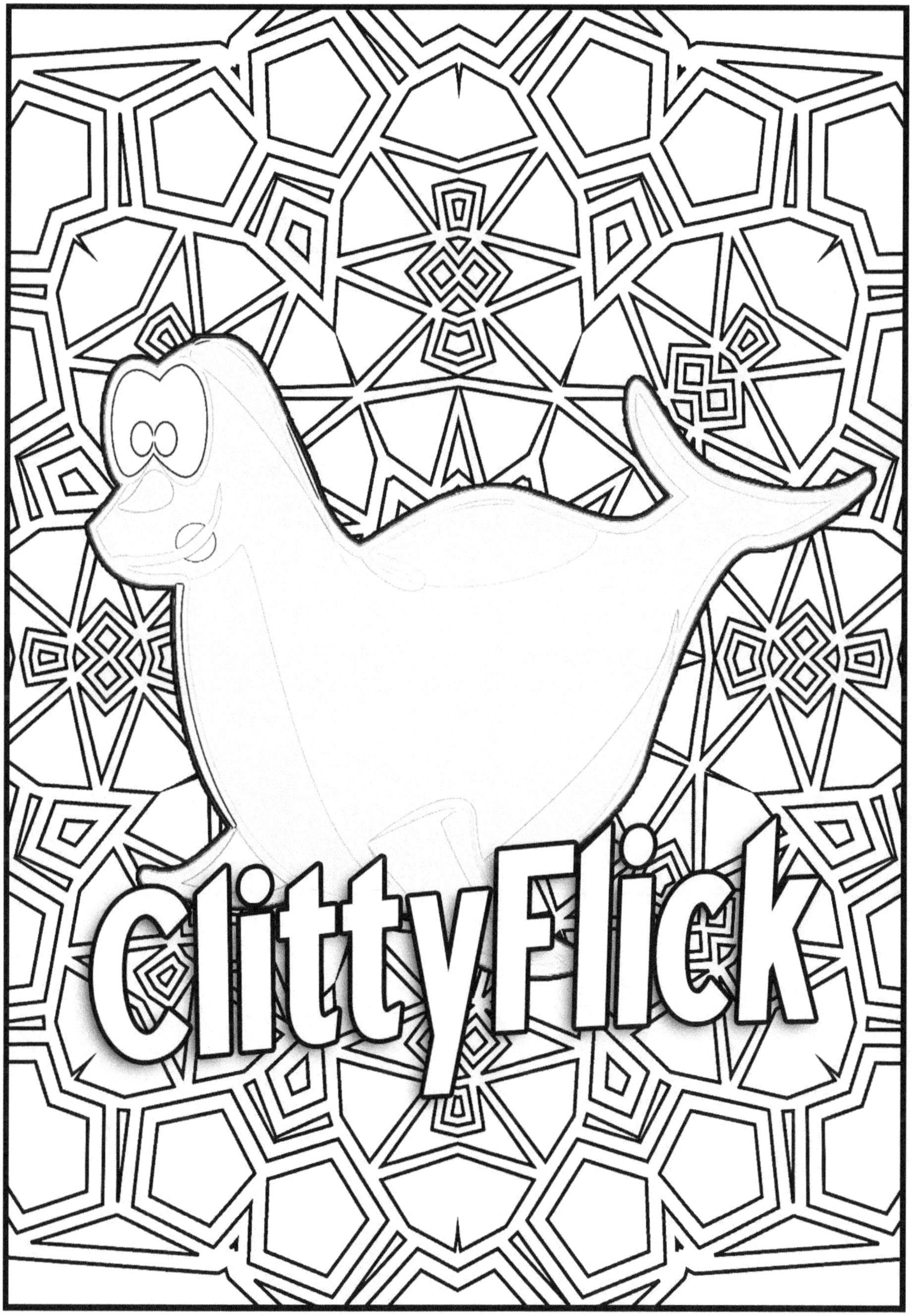
ClittyFlick

www.ingramcontent.com/pod-product-compliance
Lightning Source LLC
Chambersburg PA
CBHW080611190526
45169CB00007B/2974